✤ CONTENTS   PAGE

Furniture in the Entrance Hall is dominated by this fine carved English oak settle, dated 1694
and a white marble bust, thought to be of Queen Victoria's husband, Prince Albert.

✤ the Entrance Hall

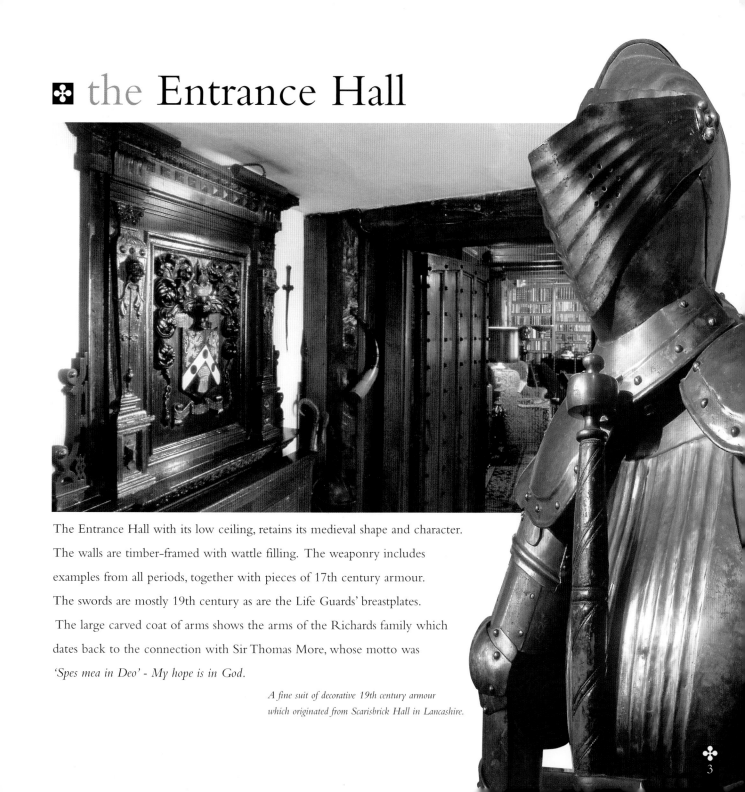

The Entrance Hall with its low ceiling, retains its medieval shape and character. The walls are timber-framed with wattle filling. The weaponry includes examples from all periods, together with pieces of 17th century armour. The swords are mostly 19th century as are the Life Guards' breastplates. The large carved coat of arms shows the arms of the Richards family which dates back to the connection with Sir Thomas More, whose motto was *'Spes mea in Deo'* - *My hope is in God.*

A fine suit of decorative 19th century armour which originated from Scarisbrick Hall in Lancashire.

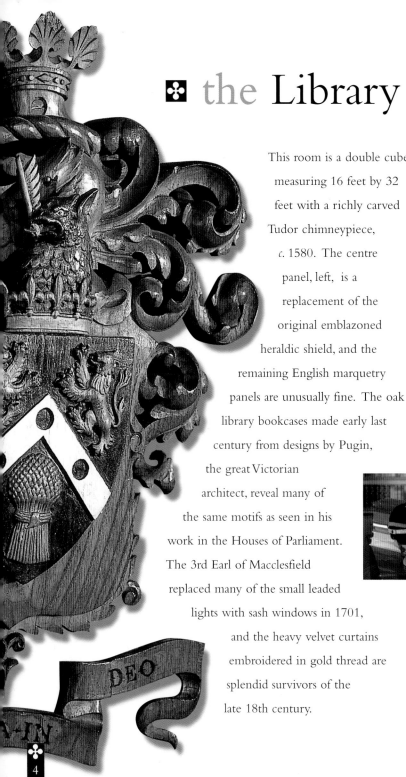

✤ the Library

This room is a double cube measuring 16 feet by 32 feet with a richly carved Tudor chimneypiece, *c.* 1580. The centre panel, left, is a replacement of the original emblazoned heraldic shield, and the remaining English marquetry panels are unusually fine. The oak library bookcases made early last century from designs by Pugin, the great Victorian architect, reveal many of the same motifs as seen in his work in the Houses of Parliament. The 3rd Earl of Macclesfield replaced many of the small leaded lights with sash windows in 1701, and the heavy velvet curtains embroidered in gold thread are splendid survivors of the late 18th century.

An early 20th century Italian cast bronze figurine of Narcissus provides a focal point on the top of the piano. Almost every printed book dealing with Cheshire (topographically and historically), finds a place on the library shelves.

The period motor racing helmet and goggles reflect the Richards' family interest in sports car racing; the English hand-built Morgan being a particular favourite.

The flint axe head *c.* 2000 B.C. displayed in the corner cabinet, was ploughed up in the park in 1912 and points to the existence of a Neolithic community living at Gawsworth in Stone Age times.

A detail from the painting by Sir David Wilkie depicting a scene at an English country inn in the early 19th century.

The richly carved coffer dated 1650 supports the figure of St. Barbara, an early 13th century French carving thought to be from the Province of Chartres, and carved from a single piece of oak. St. Barbara is the patron saint of architects and builders.

✤ the Long Hall

The Long Hall facing the western side of the courtyard retains its original fireplace and low Tudor ceiling. Interesting pieces of furniture include two heavily carved 17th century oak chests and the small 15th century credence table to the left of the fireplace, sold from the Hall in 1812, and only recently recovered.

Armour and weapons.

The candle prickets flanking the fireplace are medieval and the pictures include works by Wilkie, Turner and Constable. The portraits in many of the rooms relate to the Sneyd family of Basford and Keele. Sir Edward Fitton 2nd Baronet, married Felicia Sneyd in 1640, and an additional link with Keele was forged when Raymond Richards lodged his large and important collection of muniments with the University in 1960.

✣ the Principal Staircase

The staircase, remodelled in 1920 by the Earl of Harrington from the designs of Jabez and Percy Wright, incorporates a good deal of its original oak.

The beautiful Waterford glass chandelier *c.* 1780 is suspended above. It is fitted for 17 lights and was recently wired for electricity. The large portrait of the 1st Earl of Harrington by Allan Ramsay was acquired in 1964 when the contents of Elvaston Castle, Derby, the Earl's principal seat, were sold.

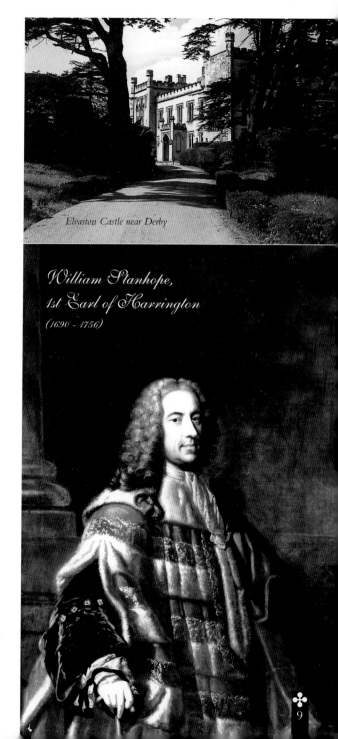

Elvaston Castle near Derby

William Stanhope,
1st Earl of Harrington
(1690 - 1756)

The Landing

The portrait of the 1st Earl of
Harrington by Allan Ramsay

The three-light East window of the Chapel depicts the Crucifixion.

✤ the Chapel and Ambulatory

The door to the south of the staircase leads into the Chapel, first mentioned by name in the Charter of 1365 when a licence was granted in December of that year for '*the administration of a domestic chapel within the house of John Fitton of Gawsworth*'. Following the canonization of Sir Thomas More by Pope Pius XI in 1935, the chapel was dedicated to his honour.

The present building is thought to be the third or possibly the fourth chapel to serve the Hall, and dates in part from the remodelling of 1701. It is a simple structure purely domestic in character. The panelled roof and pine wainscoting date from 1803, whilst the beautiful holy table and altar rails, obviously the work of the same wood carver, display the motif of running vine with elegant foliage. A particularly interesting piece of furniture is the 18th century double *prie-dieu*. The large painting – '*The Descent from the Cross*' is an early copy of the Rubens in Antwerp painted only 40 years after the artist's death.

The chapel ornaments were brought to Gawsworth from a redundant church in Ipswich, being a poor substitute for the splendid plate known to have existed in Tudor times. In April 1632, the last Sir Edward Fitton wrote to his kinsman, Sir John Trevor, that he may have to consider '*sellinge of my stocke of plate and juells*', or the plate may have been removed following the death of the 3rd Earl of Macclesfield in 1702. The two marble plaques are by Thomas Thornycroft (1815-1885), the Gawsworth sculptor who made the statue of Boadicea on Westminster Bridge. The relief of his mother bears the inscription '*Ann Thornycroft by her son 1837*'. The chapel glass is interesting. The east window of three lights depicts the Crucifixion, and the subject of the south window is Moses lifting up the brazen serpent.

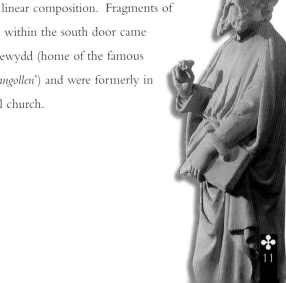

Marble relief of Ann Thornycroft by her son Thomas Thornycroft

The baptistry or ambulatory contains four lights of stained glass by William Morris (1834 - 1896), to the design of Burne-Jones. They depict St. Agnes, St. George, St. Stephen and St. Alban. William Morris and his circle were responsible for the great flowering of stained glass in the 19th century. The windows to the east of the font are classic examples of a special commission by William Morris, showing the splendid rood of three lights each with intricate foliage. His colour sense throughout is bold and sensitive, revealing a fine linear composition. Fragments of ancient glass within the south door came from Plas Newydd (home of the famous '*Ladies of Llangollen*') and were formerly in the medieval church.

✣ the Dining Room

The Dining Room to the South of the Long Hall is largely unchanged since Tudor times, with a window on the East wall looking into the Chapel. The principal piece of furniture in this room is the fine 16th century refectory table, standing on eight bulbous legs, leaf-carved with fluted domes and plain stretcher rails. The alcove by the fireplace houses examples of Wedgwood green-glazed majolica ware, manufactured about 1830. This Gawsworth dessert service has been in almost continuous use by the family since the time of its manufacture over one hundred years ago. It is surprising so much survives!

The oak escritoire is also a fine example of about 1650, the interior having fitted drawers enclosed by a heavy panelled fall front, the frieze drawer above having bold vine-leaf carving.

An arrangement of Wedgewood majolica ware in the Dining Room.

♣ the Story of *'Maggoty' Johnson*

The lion-headed fiddle in the Dining Room is thought to have been used by Samuel Johnson, the Gawsworth jester, more commonly known as Maggoty Johnson. 'Maggoty' was dancing master to the Harrington children and one of the last jesters in England in addition to being an actor and playwright. His pseudonym was 'Lord Flame', the main character in his own play 'Hurlothrumbo' which ran for 50 nights at the Haymarket Theatre in London, even the great Henry Fielding mentions it in 'Tom Jones'. Many people visited him at Gawsworth, attracted by his eccentric and reckless behaviour, and his notorious drunkeness. After one wild drinking bout his fellow actors put him in the village stocks to teach him a lesson and to let him cool off. This indignity, suffered before the eyes of the local gentry, led him to become a recluse. Towards the end of his life he financed the founding of the famous firm of Justerini and Brooks, wine-merchants, now best known for their J & B Rare Whisky. He is buried in a secluded spot known as 'Maggoty's Wood'. The grave is difficult to find but worth a visit.

The small room next to the Dining Room is known as the Guard Room - an echo of its former use in centuries past. The two chairs date from the 17th century and the blunderbuss was naval issue in the 18th century.

♣ the Drawing Room

The principal apartment to the west of the Guard Room is the Drawing Room almost unaltered since the mid 16th century. Much of the glass is original and the timbering throughout is unrestored with the exception of the oak doors which were replaced earlier this century. The Drawing Room has always been the principal living room of the hall, and today after the passing of five centuries of history, the selfsame windows look out over the same unchanged park land, still encompassed by the great Tudor wall erected by Sir Edward Fitton in the 16th century.

A corner of the Drawing Room.

The 7th Earl of Harrington was addicted to playing and
making violins; the violin displayed on the piano is a
fine example made from yew wood from the estate.
Amongst many family portraits displayed are contemporary
pastels by local artist John Mawbey of the present owners.
Two fine portraits, either side of the fireplace, are
Raymond Richards by Frank T. Copnall and
Monica Richards by Victor H. Voysey.

✣ the Gold Room

The small hall to the south of the Drawing Room gives access to the courtyard, and another door eastwards leads into the Gold Room. This room was formerly the steward's or agent's office and was used extensively up to the time of the discontinuance of the ancient Manorial Court held there until the late nineteenth century. The Manorial Court Rolls date back to early medieval times.

A curious discovery was made in 1921 when following the removal of an old cupboard a skeleton was found which was afterwards interred in the churchyard. The mystery of its identity has never been solved.

A detail of the remarkably fine early 16th century plaster frieze. Dating from about 1540, the work reveals a boldly conceived design, in monochrome, of early Renaissance character depicting Tudor roses with exquisitely fashioned birds and flowers. The design is almost identical to the old plaster mural in the great bedchamber of the Palace of Holyroodhouse worked in 1537.

An unusual and fascinating view of Waters Green, Macclesfield in 1810, by local artist James Daniel.

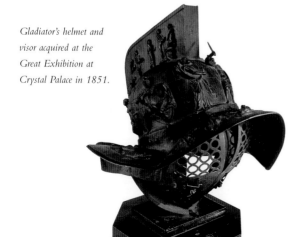

Gladiator's helmet and visor acquired at the Great Exhibition at Crystal Palace in 1851.

❧ the Green Room

The site of the original Great Hall which was reduced in size in 1701. Originally this room would have extended south as far as the yew hedge and overlooked the Tilting Ground. The picture over the fireplace is of Gawsworth Rectory by Charles Tattersall Dodd and the Minton china in the alcove, part of a complete dinner service of 120 pieces.

✤ the Gallery

Leaving the Green Room and the ground floor apartments, the Gallery is reached by the staircase which is situated at the eastern end of the Guard Room. The involved timber structure of the Gallery reveals all manner of complicated oak framing in its construction, the centre cambered beam being only six feet above floor level.

Two hiding places are constructed in the roof space; indeed the whole of the roof area lends itself admirably for this purpose. An escape hatch in the floor above conceals a narrow winding passage which descends to the cellars from which a tunnel runs under the rookery to the Church. It is thought that these hidden places date from early in the reign of Elizabeth I.
Until dispossessed of the property in 1663, Sir Alexander Fitton, a devout Roman Catholic, is believed to have maintained his own chaplain for his private devotions.

The Gallery with a portrait of
the 9th Earl of Harrington.

✤ the Solar

The Solar originally extended outwards, conforming to the same plan as the Green Room beneath.
The extensive reduction in the size of the hall which took place in 1701, resulted in the large timbered truss by the windows overlooking the park becoming very much out of proportion in relation to the apartment as a whole. Originally this room would have been three times its present size.

In 1693 Lord Macclesfield complained that the old house at Gawsworthy was ready to fall upon his head. This no doubt was an exaggeration, but certainly his son, Fitton Gerard, 3rd Earl of Macclesfield, left nothing to chance and had the decayed parts pulled down in 1701, a month before his own death on Christmas Day.

With his death the baronies of Gerard and Brandon and the earldom of Macclesfield became extinct, and Lady Mohun, granddaughter of the first Earl, came into possession of the estates - an uneasy heritage which culminated in the notorious duel of 1712 between the Duke of Hamilton and Lord Mohun. The focal point of the room is a four-poster bed dating from the 16th century known as the Boswell bed. It belonged at one time to the Boswell family who added their arms to the covering board. The bed, with its richly elaborated marquetry tester and boldly carved bed head, would be well known to Boswell, the diarist and biographer of Dr. Johnson. It came to Gawsworth from Lympne Castle in Kent. From the window there is a good view of the lower Pennine range of hills with Shutlingslow, 1,659 feet, and the Cloud at Bosley, 1,190 feet above sea level, being prominent features. The tall lighthouse structure seen on the summit of Sutton Common is a Post Office tower completed in 1963. Although modern in design, it is now an acceptable part of the general landscape.

Charles, 4th Baron Mohun
by Sir Godfrey Kneller, 1707.

By Courtesy of The National Portrait Gallery, London.

Mohun fought his first duel at the age of 15. A few days later he was involved in the brutal murder of an actor, but was acquitted. After a subsequent duel and a fatal stabbing, where, on both occasions, he walked free from trial, he finally met his end in a duel with the Duke of Hamilton in London's Hyde Park, but not before killing the Duke with his shortened sword as his opponent bent over him.

♣ the
Hall
Room

The principal bedroom of the house with its rich windowing and ancient stone fireplace is a splendid survival of this part of the building dating from the early 16th century. The oak framing, wainscoting, flooring, plaster work and glass are quite unchanged since Tudor times. Here Fittons were born and Fittons died. Lady Adderley, the remarried widow of the last Fitton Baronet, whose end is so poignantly described in Henry Newcombe's diary, died here in 1650.

In 1683 the Duke of Monmouth slept in this room and possibly at an earlier date, his father, King Charles II. A succession of the Earls of Harrington knew the hall and this bedroom, until the property passed out of the family in 1955. The Prince Regent's friend, Viscount Petersham, lived at the hall from time to time in the early 19th century, and no doubt in this room he dreamed of new ideas of dazzling his Royal master who visited him on two occasions at Gawsworth.

Lord Petersham is remembered for his famous Cossack trousers, and the splendid double-breasted coat named after him which outshone the famous dandy of the age, '*Beau*' Brummell. Lord Petersham's 'snuff-cellar' was well known, and he owned no less than 365 superb snuffboxes, one for each day of the year.

A great four-poster bed has always been the focal furnishing feature of this chamber, and the present example is an exceptionally large bed dating from the time of William and Mary.

The fine portrait on the west wall portrays Anne, Lady Fitton, aged thirty-eight, her son Edward (later the second and last baronet), aged six, and his sister Mary, aged seven. This portrait was for many years at Brereton Hall, where it was seen and carefully documented by Ormerod when compiling his history of Cheshire early last century. Ormerod's letters and interesting heraldic notes concerning this picture are now preserved with the Gawsworth papers. The shield of arms on the portrait are those of Fitton impaling Barret, bearing on a shield of pretence those of Holcroft.

Detail from:

Anne,
Lady Fitton

with her children,
Edward and Mary,
1609.

✤ Mary Fitton's Bedroom

From the Hall Bedroom, one looks through the former powder and dressing room, now remodelled into a modern bathroom, and glimpses the Fitton Bedroom. This small apartment has lovely old plaster elaboration in the frieze, and considerable amounts of old timber-framing are also exposed.

♣ the French Room

Moving from the Gallery northwards, visitors enter the French Room, with its elegantly carved 18th century French bed, mirrored in the picture to the right.

♣ the Staircase and Passage

This room in turn gives access to the principal staircase. The Northern Passage reveals some of the massive oak trusses which carry the roof structure. Many of the pictures are the work of the celebrated Riseley family of Gawsworth.

♣ the Griffin Room

The small bedroom, facing north and known as the Griffin Room, has a Tudor squared plaster ceiling. The elegantly carved linenfold oak door on the west side of this room leads to the Billiard Room.

♣ the Billiard Room

The exposed roof timbers can be seen in detail in this part of the Hall and with the exception of the two boxed-in tie rods, the structure is late 15th century.

The reclining marble figure of a young girl '*Echo*', is by Alfred Gatley, the Macclesfield Kerridge Sculptor (1816 - 1863), signed and dated 1853. Here also is his bust of the poet Milton signed and dated 1835.

The sculptor's portrait was painted in Rome the year before his death, signed and dated '*Marcianno da Tuna, Roma 1862*'. Preserved in the house with the Gatley family papers are his diary and letter books.

'Echo'
by Alfred Gatley,
signed and dated 1853

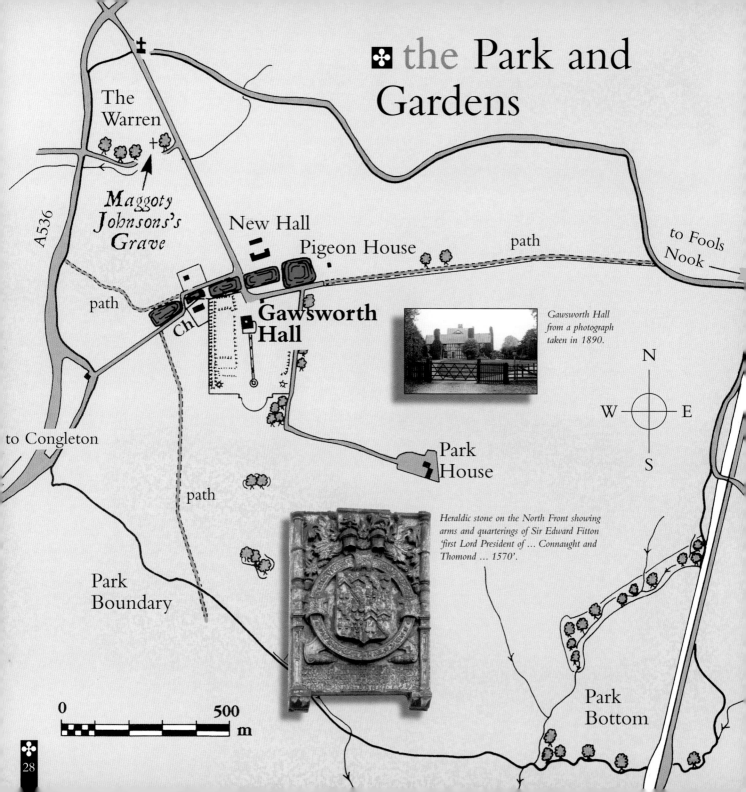

♣ the Park and Gardens

The Warren

Maggoty Johnsons's Grave

A536

New Hall

Pigeon House

path

to Fools Nook

path

Ch.

Gawsworth Hall

Gawsworth Hall from a photograph taken in 1890.

N

W   E

S

to Congleton

path

Park House

Heraldic stone on the North Front showing arms and quarterings of Sir Edward Fitton 'first Lord President of … Connaught and Thomond … 1570'.

Park Boundary

Park Bottom

0   500 m

Leaving the Hall by the North door, a flight of stone steps from the garden, leads up to the ancient rookery and on to the Tilting Ground, which formed part of a vast Elizabethan pleasure garden. Built by Sir Edward Fitton in the late 16th century to rival such great gardens as Holdenby, Sir Edward obviously hoped for a visit by Queen Elizabeth I on a royal progress. The Tudor wall and the massive earthworks can still be seen and are all that remains of the formal terracing and planting. This inner garden of approximately 30 acres was set within a larger park of nearly 600 acres, a vast private estate for the enjoyment of the Fittons and their guests. Even the village was moved from around the Church and the Hall to its present site.

An idea of the usage of the garden comes from a description of the visit of the Duke of Monmouth to Gawsworth, almost a century later, in 1682. '*Upon Friday, September 15th, the Duke of Monmouth came attended by a considerable number of gentlemen to the Earl of Macclesfield's house at Gawsworth, and that the company called upon ye rabble to shout*'. The following day, Saturday the 16th, there was buck-shooting in Lord Macclesfield's park, followed by a great banquet and some sweetmeats were received by one of the witnesses, distributed to him and to others by the Earl's own hand. On the same day, "*upon a plaine neare to ye Earl's house*" a game called a Prison-barrplay was performed by 20 young men, for which a piece of plate was presented by Lord Macclesfield. They were afterwards given five guineas for making the Duke that sport, another guinea being presented to two kettle-drummers of the Earl's who had assisted on this occasion. Four thousand people were supposed to have been present, and when the Duke came into the field to see the sport '*there seemed to bee great satisfaccon to ye Crowd in his presence, which ye multitude expressed by shouting*'.

Right from top: *A corner view of the Tilting Ground.*
                        The sundial incorporating an unusual chequered pavement design.
                        The Homecoming Board on the Hall exterior.
                        A view of Gawsworth Hall from the North across the Lake.

Far left: Excavations in 1989 - 1990, indicating seating and left, part of the terracing on the North slope of the great linear bank.

THE TILTING GROUND was divided into several different sections. On the western side is a long bank, running directly in a north-south direction. Excavation underneath the turf reveals a wide gravel path. Obviously the bank was intended to be a walkway for ladies in delicate shoes. The wall here is only at eye level - giving those within the garden marvellous views over the Cheshire plain to the west, and towards the Pennines in the east. The flat plateau next to the Rookery was surrounded by a high wall and was what the Elizabethans would have called a Wilderness Garden. The grass banks to the south of the plateau give the impression of seating but excavation has revealed a different story. On the north side, the terrace slopes below the main plateau, were themselves revetted by a brick wall. Behind each wall was evidence of a flower bed and a turfed walk.

Unfortunately, all these walls were removed in the early 19th century possibly to provide bricks for repairs to the outer wall. The identical earthworks on the western side show no signs of any brick revettment - this side has always been a stepped turfed slope but here evidence was found of symmetrically and regularly planted trees. Excavation in the low central section of the garden has revealed that it was sealed with red clay. Old maps show a system of sluices and it may have originally been possible to flood the central section of the garden to make a large shallow ornamental lake.

Sir Edward Fitton may have intended to emulate the water entertainments used at Elvetham and Kenilworth to entertain the Queen. Mary Fitton, as a maid of honour, would certainly have been present at these occasions and been able to tell her parents of their success. The survival of the remains of this garden results from a series of accidents of history: after Mary's disgrace from court, the Fitton finances never recovered. At the end of the Civil War, a long legal battle began between Sir Charles Gerard, later the 1st Earl of Macclesfield, and Alexander Fitton over the Gawsworth estates. This was finally settled in 1663 but events came to a head again in 1701 with the death of Fitton Gerard, 3rd Earl of Macclesfield, who left no male heirs. The estate was left to a niece, Lady Mohun and was contested by another niece, the Duchess of Hamilton. The dispute culminated in the famous duel of 1712 between Lord Mohun and the Duke of Hamilton where both combatants were killed! Lord Harrington bought the estate in 1725 but he kept his main residence at Elvaston Castle near Derby and only visited the Hall occasionally. Thus for almost three hundred years Gawsworth remained untouched, escaping the hands of Capability Brown and remaining undisturbed by the passing whims of landscape designers.

✤ the Fittons

In 1316 Isabel de Orreby married Thomas Fitton of Boleyn and from these inauspicious beginnings started the most famous family to live at Gawsworth. Originally the family lived in a wooden stockaded building in the Rookery but around 1480 the present house was built similar in style and size to nearby Little Moreton Hall.

During the Wars of the Roses another Thomas Fitton fought and was knighted at the battle of Blore Heath near Market Drayton when 31 of his 66 men were killed. The Fittons were typical of so many Tudor families – Knights and farmers elevated under the Tudor kings as a consequence of the Wars of the Roses. Henry VII was a shrewd, cautious man who fought hard for the throne and was determined there would be no repeat of the previous twenty years of war. The power of the great families was ruthlessly pruned. The third Sir Edward Fitton was knighted in 1566 and appointed Lord President of Connaught and Thomond in 1569. His affairs brought him in contact with William Cecil, Lord Burghley and all the great Officers of State. He would read aloud the Queen's letter of June 1572 written from Greenwich observing that she had received a letter complaining of Fitton's haughty countenance and contempt for his superiors, this was displeasing to hear, '*and that she would have Fitton repute it praise and honour to have suffered trouble for doing Her Majesty good service*'.

The third Sir Edward Fitton succeeded his father in 1579 and was equally distinguished, holding office for some years as Lord President of Munster. He married Alice, daughter of Sir John Holcroft, and many of her letters survive, particularly those written to her two famous daughters, Anne and Mary. Anne married Sir John Newdegate of Arbury and Mary, through her father's influence at Court, was appointed in 1596 Maid of Honour to Queen Elizabeth I. Famed for her beauty, Mary Fitton is the supposed '*Dark Lady*' of Shakespeare's sonnets. It is not without the bounds of possibility that Shakespeare himself came to Gawsworth Hall during this period when journeying to Rufford.

by courtesy of Arbury Hall

Mary Fitton's short but brilliant career at Court came to an untimely end in 1602 when Sir Robert Cecil reported that Mary Fitton was to bear a child and that she and the Earl of Pembroke '*would both dwell in the Tower awhile for the Queen hath vowed to send him thither*'.

Mary was sent home in disgrace and eventually joined her sister, Anne, at Arbury. It is only in the last few years that the full ramifications of her disgrace have come to light. Sir Edward Fitton had started to build a garden to rival those at Holdenby and Chipping Campden, hoping for a royal visit. The Tilting Ground and its earthworks were laid out, the Tudor wall was built, the lakes were enlarged and several avenues of lime trees were planted. Richard Turner, the Cheshire Archaeologist, suggests the cost in today's terms was some £10 million. It is no wonder Sir Edward Fitton tried so hard to make Pembroke agree to marry Mary! Mary's brother, Edward, however, regained favour with the Crown and was created a baronet in 1617. The Civil War saw great comings and goings at Gawsworth. The house must certainly have been the scene of many sad partings, particularly when Sir Edward left Gawsworth in the early spring of 1643 for ever. Fighting alongside Prince Rupert he died in August of that year.

Then followed the famous will case, the verdict enabling Sir Edward Fitton's nephew, Charles Gerard, later Lord Gerard of Brandon and Earl of Macclesfield, to recover the Gawsworth estates from Sir Alexander Fitton. Afterwards Lord Macclesfield lived at the hall in great splendour when the house was the scene of much entertaining. Previously, as Lord Gerard at the Court of King Charles II, he held the office of Gentleman of the Bedchamber and the rank of Captain of the Guard. Samuel Pepys in his diary has much to say of the events of this period and of the will case. Meantime, Sir Alexander Fitton, grandson of Sir Edward Fitton who died in 1579, although dispossessed in 1663 of the Gawsworth estates eventually found favour on the accession of James II. Always a staunch Roman Catholic, the King made him Chancellor of Ireland and after his abdication conferred upon him the title of Baron Fitton of Gawsworth. The Hall was indeed the centre of great events and its owners were never far from history in the making. The sequence of events continued with the visit of the Duke of Monmouth in 1682, and the tragic duel over the estates in 1712, when both Lord Mohun and the Duke of Hamilton perished, an event which aroused Queen Anne's wrath and her prolonged interest in Gawsworth affairs.

The Duke of Monmouth, Charles II's illegitimate son by Lucy Walter, visited Gawsworth in 1682.

✣ the Earls of Harrington to the present day

 William Stanhope was born in 1690 and by 1715 he was Colonel of a dragoon regiment and had entered Parliament as the Whig member for Derby. Evidently gifted as a diplomat, he was Ambassador to Spain both before and after the Spanish war and was created Earl of Harrington in 1742. About 1718, he married the second Lady Mohun's daughter, Anne Griffiths, and he purchased the estates at Gawsworth in 1725 following the death of Lady Mohun. **William Stanhope, 2nd Earl**, was like his father both a soldier and politician attaining the rank of General in 1770. **Charles Stanhope, 3rd Earl**, was also a soldier and travelled widely in his army career with tours of duty in America during the War of Independence and in the West Indies. By 1792 he was Colonel of the 1st Life Guards when he introduced a new type of sword which was then adopted by the whole British army. Later he retired from army life to plan the rebuilding of Elvaston Castle and Harrington House in Kensington. George III and Queen Charlotte were frequent visitors to Harrington House and the tea-drinking parties there. Jane Countess of Harrington was a Lady of the Bedchamber and a great favourite of the Queen. The 3rd Earl's son, **Charles, Viscount Petersham**, was in his late forties when he succeeded to the title. '*Beau*' Petersham, as he was known, had a reputation as a Regency buck. A trendsetter who rivalled '*Beau*' Brummel, he was a friend of the Prince Regent and was well known for tea drinking and taking snuff. Tall and handsome, he gave his name to the Petersham overcoat and the Harrington hat! His love affair with Maria Foote, an actress considerably younger than himself, was the talk of London society of the time and was disapproved of greatly by his father. After his father's death the 4th Earl married the actress and took his bride back to Elvaston where he started to transform the park and grounds with the help of William Barron, a Scotsman, who had trained at the Botanical Gardens in Edinburgh. Under his direction a series of theme gardens began to take shape - an Italian garden, a Moorish garden and a Topiary garden. For twenty years the Harringtons lived at Elvaston in their private world, whilst around them the gardens matured that were to make Elvaston famous. Indeed on the death in 1851 of the 4th Earl, his brother the 5th Earl opened Elvaston to the public with an entrance fee of 3/-. Such was the reputation of the gardens that people flocked in their thousands to see them.

Leicester Stanhope, the 5th Earl, is famous for his association with the poet Byron. In 1823 he went to Missolonghi in Greece where he set up a newspaper and opened a school. Lord

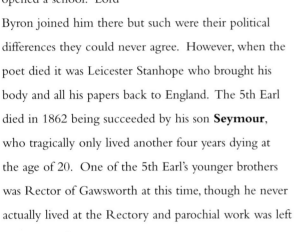

The 8th Earl of Harrington, 'Old Whiskers'

Byron joined him there but such were their political differences they could never agree. However, when the poet died it was Leicester Stanhope who brought his body and all his papers back to England. The 5th Earl died in 1862 being succeeded by his son **Seymour**, who tragically only lived another four years dying at the age of 20. One of the 5th Earl's younger brothers was Rector of Gawsworth at this time, though he never actually lived at the Rectory and parochial work was left to a series of curates.

After Seymour Stanhope's death, the title passed to a cousin, **Charles Wyndham Stanhope**. The **7th Earl**, whose portrait hangs at Gawsworth, was passionately interested in the making and playing of violins. The violin in the Drawing Room at Gawsworth is a fine example, made from Elvaston yew and displaying the Harrington cypher on the back. Sadly the Earl died as a result of a wood-working accident.

Charles Augustus Stanhope, the **8th Earl**, was known as *Old Whiskers* because of his bushy white beard. A former cavalry officer he loved horses and was a keen huntsman. Charles Augustus lived in the New Hall at Gawsworth between 1869 - 1881 while he was Viscount Petersham. He was Lieut. Col. Commander of the Cheshire Imperial Yeomanry until 1881 when he became the 8th Earl. He left instructions in his will that the hounds were to hunt on the first suitable day after his death. The day after the funeral the hounds set off across the park at Elvaston. They raced to the churchyard where, to the amazement of the hunt, they gathered round their late Master's grave. A qualified civil engineer he maintained an engineering workshop at Elvaston and died from blood poisoning in 1917. Local rumour was that his fatal accident was the result of trying to make a bomb for the war effort!

Dudley Stanhope, his brother, became **9th Earl** and was succeeded by his grandson **Charles** in 1927. Tragically the 10th Earl died two years later in 1929, the result of a fall from his horse in the hunting field. His son, **William**, is the present **Earl of Harrington** who lives in Ireland.

Lady Philippa, the sister of the 8th and 9th Earls lived at Gawsworth at the end of the 19th century, marrying William Waithman of Merlin Park, Co. Galway in 1883.

The Hon. Julia Vereker with her groom and maid on a visit to Gawsworth in 1897.

1918 and 1920 renovating the Hall and modernising it. Jabez Wright the well-known Macclesfield architect and Lord Harrington's agent were in charge of the work and oversaw the removal of the blue slate roof and re-roofing it in stone slates, the replacement of the Victorian conservatory with the Library oriel window and the building of the new kitchen wing. The Shimwells remained at Gawsworth until the mid 1930s when Dennis de Ferranti and his family took over the tenure of the Hall. The Richards family moved to the Hall in 1962. Raymond Richards, the well-known Cheshire historian, had previously lived at the Old Rectory and it was to him that Lord Harrington made over the Lordship of the Manor and Patronage of the Living when he moved to Ireland. Raymond and Monica Richards restored the Hall to its former splendour and opened the house to the public in 1966. Timothy and Elizabeth Richards have carried on this tradition since 1981. They have seen their family grow up at the Hall and are continuing the task of maintaining one of Cheshire's best-loved manor houses and continuing the tradition of summer entertainment in the Open Air Theatre.

The Hall was empty during the First World War when the Household Cavalry used the Tilting Ground to train horses and mules to canon fire before leaving for France to join the army. The mules were wild and Ernest Bayley, who lived in Gawsworth all his life, clearly remembered the night when four mules bolted up the Congleton Road, overturning the waggon they were pulling on the Gawsworth crossroads and not stopping until they returned to the stables at the Hall! The Shimwell family became tenants in 1918. Captain Shimwell, a wealthy jute manufacturer in Manchester, and Lord Harrington spent a total of £22,000 between

Armorial tablet to Raymond Richards (1906 - 1978) in Gawsworth Church.

❖ Gawsworth today

Gawsworth is now the home of Timothy and Elizabeth Richards and since 1969 they have developed a unique Open Air Theatre venue. There are few more satisfying sights than the spectacle of this old house as the backdrop to summer theatre and music, attracting visitors from far and wide.

Over the years the list of artists and performers reads like a who's who of the arts and entertainment world: Rolf Harris, Elkie Brooks, Kenny Ball, Marion Montgomery, Acker Bilk, Sir John Mortimer, Honor Blackman, and a host of opera and classical music stars. More recently Gawsworth has extended its repertoire and is now able to provide excellent facilities for weddings and receptions, and regularly holds other stimulating events throughout the year, including the Classic Car Rally, the Antique and Collectors Fairs and regular Craft Fairs. Over the Festive Season there are additional events such as Yuletide at Christmas.

For all details telephone 01260 223456

The Gondoliers

Open Air Theatre - 1969